Curriculum Visions

Spaceship Earth

WITHDRAWN

Dr Brian Knapp

Glossary

ASH

Fragments of lava that have cooled and solidified between when they leave a volcano and when they fall to the surface.

ASTEROID

Any of the many small objects within the Solar System. Asteroids are rocky or metallic and are conventionally described as significant bodies with a diameter smaller than 1,000 km.

ATMOSPHERE

The envelope of gases that surrounds the Earth and other bodies in the Universe.

CONSERVE

To save or preserve something so it can be used for a long time.

CORE

The central region of a body. The core of the Earth is about 3,300 km in radius, compared with the radius of the whole Earth, which is 6,300 km.

CRATER

A deep bowl-shaped depression in the surface of a body formed by the high-speed impact of another, smaller body.

CRUST

The solid outer surface of a rocky body. The crust of the Earth is mainly just a few tens of kilometres thick, compared to the total radius of 6,300 km for the whole Earth.

ECLIPSE

The time when light is cut off by a body coming between the observer and the source of the illumination (for example, eclipse of the Sun), or when the body the observer is on comes between the source of illumination and another body (for example, eclipse of the Moon).

ENERGY

The ability to make things happen.

FOSSIL FUELS

A fuel produced from plants or animals long ago that is found in the Earth's crust. The main fossil fuels are coal, gas and oil.

GAS

Material in the form of vapour, like air.

GRAVITY

The force of attraction between bodies. The larger an object, the more its gravitational pull on other objects. The Sun's gravity is the most powerful in the Solar System, keeping all of the planets and other materials within the Solar System.

HURRICANE

A very violent cyclone that begins close to the equator, and that contains winds of over 117 km/hr.

LAVA

Hot, melted rock from a volcano. Lava flows onto the surface of a planet and cools and hardens to form new rock. Most of the lava on Earth is made of basalt.

MOLTEN

A solid which has become liquid.

PHOTOSYNTHESIS

The process in which the green material in a plant uses the energy in sunlight to make food and oxygen from water and carbon dioxide.

POLLUTE

To make something, like the air or land, dirty and unusable.

SATELLITE

A man-made object that orbits the Earth. Usually used as a term for an unmanned spacecraft whose job is to acquire or transfer data to and from the ground.

SEASONS

The characteristic cycle of events in the heating of the Earth that causes related changes in weather patterns.

SHADOW

The shade cast when the path of light is blocked by an object.

SOLAR SYSTEM

The Sun and the bodies orbiting around it.

STEWARDSHIP

Looking after something, such as the Earth, so that it is healthy.

SUN

The star that the planets of the Solar System revolve around.

UNIVERSE

The entirety of everything there is: the cosmos. Many space scientists prefer to use the term "cosmos," referring to the entirety of energy and matter.

VOLCANO

A mound or mountain that is formed from ash or lava.

WATER VAPOUR

The gaseous form of water. Also sometimes referred to as moisture.

Contents

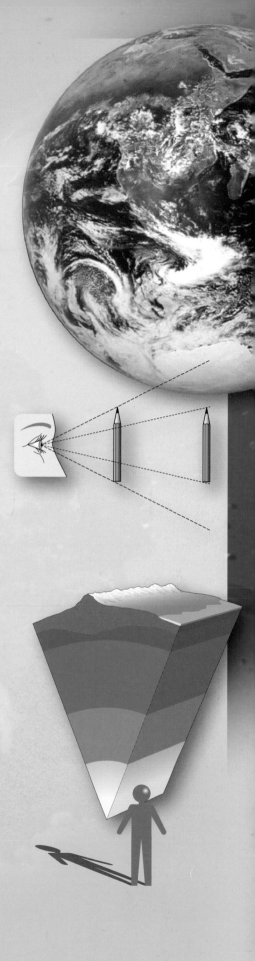

Weblink: www.CurriculumVisions.com

The Sun keeps the Earth spinning around it by the force of **GRAVITY**.

The Sun supplies the Earth with sunlight, a form of energy.

◀ ① The Earth and the Sun are connected. Without the Sun, life on the Earth could not survive.

Planet Earth Facts

◆ The Earth is about 149,573,000 km from the Sun.
◆ The Earth is the third planet from the Sun.
◆ It speeds around its orbit at nearly 30 km a second.
◆ It takes 365.25 Earth days to make a complete revolution around the Sun.
◆ The Earth spins on a tilted axis, revolving once every 23 hours, 56 minutes and 4 seconds.

Spaceship Earth

Our planet is like a giant spaceship set in the vastness of airless space. But it is not quite self sufficient because it needs the Sun to power it.

Have you ever thought of our planet as a spaceship? It is the most successful spaceship that we know of in the **UNIVERSE**. That is because it has built-in ways to survive.

Sunlight

Every spaceship needs a source of **ENERGY**. The Earth's energy comes from the Sun (picture ①). We call this energy sunlight. In sunlight are light and heat, which allow life on Earth. If the Earth were ever to drift away from the Sun, living things on our spaceship would soon die.

Air

Hugging the Earth's surface is invisible air. Its particles of **GAS** scatter some sunlight, so that we see the sky as blue.

Two gases in the air are vital for life: they are the oxygen that we breathe in (and which plants release), and the carbon dioxide which we breathe out (and plants take in).

The air has one other important role. It tends to act like an invisible blanket, holding on to some of the heat from the **SUN** and making the Earth a warm world.

Water

Water can also be a gas in the air. In this form we call it **WATER VAPOUR**. It is invisible until it turns into tiny droplets which show up as white or grey clouds

in sunlight. The moisture comes mainly from the oceans and returns to the Earth as rain. When rain falls on to land it gives the water that all living things need to survive.

Surrounding the land is the ocean (picture ②). It covers about 71% of the Earth's surface (see also page 8).

▲ ② This diagram shows some important features of the Earth. Most of the surface is covered with water, and this is also where most of the Earth's life is to be found. Some ocean water is cold (blue), while some is warm (red). Surrounding the Earth is the atmosphere and its clouds.

The temperature of the oceans, the rain from the clouds and the gases in the air are all vital in allowing life on Earth. If we disturb these natural systems, we could also destroy life on Earth.

Weblink: www.CurriculumVisions.com

How the Earth formed

The Earth, affectionately known as the 'Blue Marble', is streaked with clouds of water in the atmosphere. As far as we know there is no other planet like it.

 **(1) The formation of the Earth.**

1 The earliest Earth collected as a mass of gas which collapsed under the force of gravity. Nuclear reactions inside this material released further heat and caused the core to become molten.

2 After a billion years the surface had cooled and developed a crust of solid rocks. At the same time, the surface was bombarded with meteorites that made huge craters, just like those seen on the Moon today. Hot rock inside the Earth was continually turned over, dragging the crust apart and allowing vast sheets of molten rock (lava) to flow out and cool to make more crust. This process is still happening today.

3 As the crust thickened and less lava flowed to the surface there was an opportunity for some gases to condense and form the water of the oceans and the atmosphere.

4 Life forms probably developed first in the hot liquids near volcanic eruptions. Slowly, the developing plant life helped to absorb carbon dioxide and release oxygen, changing the composition of the air and allowing life to colonise the land.

The Earth first formed at the same time as the Sun and the other planets, about 4.6 billion years ago (picture ①).

It grew by taking more and more dust from space. The bigger it became, the more the dust squashed together, releasing heat and making the whole planet **MOLTEN**.

Once the dust was used up, the Earth stopped growing and the surface cooled to form the **CRUST**. The crust acted like an insulating blanket around the core, to keep the Earth's **CORE** molten (picture ②).

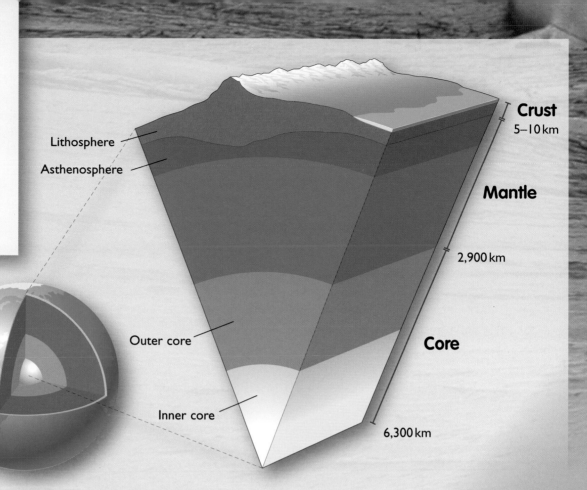

Lithosphere

Asthenosphere

Outer core

Inner core

Crust
5–10 km

Mantle

2,900 km

Core

6,300 km

▲ ② The Earth is made of many rocky layers. The surface layer – the crust – is cold and hard. The layer below – the mantle – is hot and moves, crushing up the surface crust to make mountain ranges.

The inside of the Earth – the core – is mostly molten iron. As it churns about it makes a giant magnet that gives us our north and south poles.

The importance of volcanoes

VOLCANOES are the main way that heat and materials escape from inside the Earth.

Volcanoes do not just send out **LAVA** and **ASH**, they also belch out gases such as oxygen, **WATER VAPOUR**, nitrogen and carbon dioxide. This is what has formed the air, the clouds and the oceans (picture ③).

▼ ③ Volcanoes have created our atmosphere.

Air, water and life

The Earth contains water and air. These are needed for life.

The Earth contains large amounts of oxygen in the air and liquid water. About 21% of the air is oxygen and about 71% of the Earth's surface is covered with ocean. This is quite unlike any other planet in the Solar System.

Life started in water

In the early Earth there was no oxygen in the air. This is how it got to be there.

Life first started in the water. This is why space scientists look for signs of water on planets like Mars. If you find liquid water, you are likely to find life.

The first life was very small and very simple. The first large living things were water plants. We call them algae. Eventually plants grew on land, too.

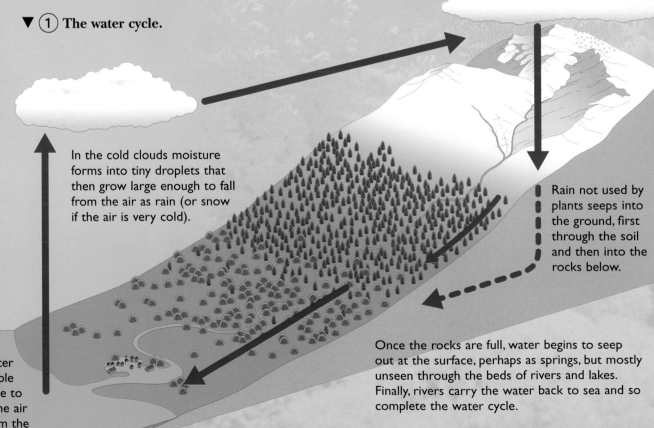

▼ ① **The water cycle.**

When rain falls, most of it immediately sinks into the soil. Plants suck up water from the soil through their roots.

Snow falls in cold weather and may remain on the ground until spring. If it melts quickly, it may swell rivers and cause floods.

In the cold clouds moisture forms into tiny droplets that then grow large enough to fall from the air as rain (or snow if the air is very cold).

Rain not used by plants seeps into the ground, first through the soil and then into the rocks below.

Liquid ocean water changes to invisible water vapour due to the warmth of the air and the heat from the Sun. This is known as evaporation.

Once the rocks are full, water begins to seep out at the surface, perhaps as springs, but mostly unseen through the beds of rivers and lakes. Finally, rivers carry the water back to sea and so complete the water cycle.

Plants release oxygen

All plants use a substance called carbon dioxide gas to grow. It is an invisible gas found in water and air. It is made of carbon and oxygen. But plants do not need all of the oxygen in carbon dioxide and so they release it.

As a result oxygen is released into the water and the air.

▼ ② The carbon cycle.

Animals need plants

Animals in water and on land need oxygen to live. They also need plants to eat. Animals, including ourselves, rely on plants for survival. We always will.

Cycles

Spaceship Earth reuses its precious materials: water, carbon and oxygen, the things we need for life. Pictures ① and ② show how water, carbon and oxygen are recycled.

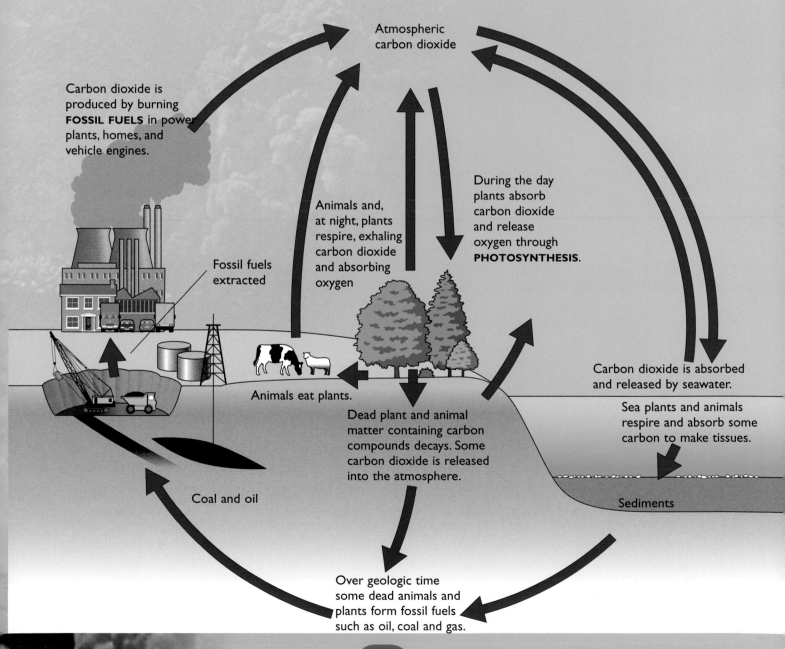

Atmospheric carbon dioxide

Carbon dioxide is produced by burning **FOSSIL FUELS** in power plants, homes, and vehicle engines.

Fossil fuels extracted

Animals and, at night, plants respire, exhaling carbon dioxide and absorbing oxygen

During the day plants absorb carbon dioxide and release oxygen through **PHOTOSYNTHESIS**.

Animals eat plants.

Carbon dioxide is absorbed and released by seawater.

Sea plants and animals respire and absorb some carbon to make tissues.

Dead plant and animal matter containing carbon compounds decays. Some carbon dioxide is released into the atmosphere.

Coal and oil

Sediments

Over geologic time some dead animals and plants form fossil fuels such as oil, coal and gas.

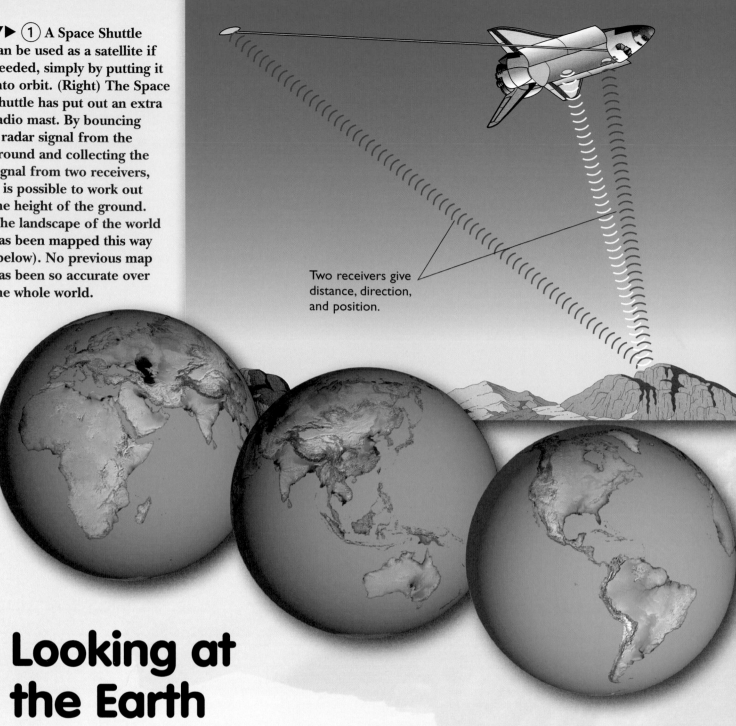

① A Space Shuttle can be used as a satellite if needed, simply by putting it into orbit. (Right) The Space Shuttle has put out an extra radio mast. By bouncing a radar signal from the ground and collecting the signal from two receivers, it is possible to work out the height of the ground. The landscape of the world has been mapped this way (below). No previous map has been so accurate over the whole world.

Two receivers give distance, direction, and position.

Looking at the Earth

Satellites can see the world and give us information in ways we never had before.

Think of the daily weather forecast on television. Most of the images, and much of the information the weather forecaster needs, comes from **SATELLITES**.

Satellites can also tell us about places where there are hurricanes, or fires or floods (picture ②). They can spot erupting volcanoes (picture ②), they can measure the height of the land (picture ①) or the temperature of the sea. They can work out different kinds of rock and see which kinds of forest are healthy and where the trees are dying (picture ②).

Satellite Facts

- Satellites that look at the Earth do not take photographs – they take digital images.
- Scientists get even more information by 'looking' at the Earth using radar and other kinds of signal.
- Infra-red images (such as LANDSAT) can show things such as plants that are growing well or are diseased. This helps in conservation studies.

▶ ② Satellites can give us very detailed pictures of the surface. (Top left) A picture of New York City on 9.11.2001. (Top right) A close up of the World Trade Center as it burned. (Centre) The eruption of Mt Etna, Italy. (Bottom right) Three superimposed pictures of Hurricane Andrew (1992) approaching the coast of the United States.

▲ ③ It is often better to use colour to give information. This is a LANDSAT image of the Lena River Delta in Russia. The rivers are deep blue, sandbanks are purple. All of the other colours show different kinds of forest.

Weblink: www.CurriculumVisions.com

Looking after the world

We have to learn how to look after our spaceship Earth and not use it all up or pollute it.

We only have one world: spaceship Earth. Of all the living things that have existed on the Earth, we are the only ones that have ever been able to change the world (pictures ① and ②).

Why do we change things?

Our need to eat makes us plough the land and keep cows, sheep and chickens. It makes us cut down forests and replace them with pastures and crops. It makes us fish in the world's great oceans.

Our need for energy makes us dig coal and drill for oil, build dams, flood valleys and do many other things.

Above all, we make machines and, with them, we change the world.

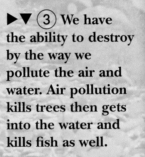

▼ ① The dodo is an example of an animal that was made extinct because of human activities.

▶▼ ③ We have the ability to destroy by the way we pollute the air and water. Air pollution kills trees then gets into the water and kills fish as well.

▼ ② We have the ability to destroy by thoughtless killing.

What change has caused

The way we live creates waste. It **POLLUTES** the land, the water and the air (picture ③). It also destroys the homes of many living things with which we share the planet.

Our responsibilities

Every living thing – including ourselves – depends on the other living things around it.

Because we have such power to destroy, we have a duty to be sensitive to other living things. This is called **STEWARDSHIP** (picture ④).

▼ ④ **We can protect our environment as neighbours in our local community, such as looking after this pond.**

If we are going to look after – **CONSERVE** – our world and not damage it or pollute it more than we can help, we have to know what we are doing wrong and how to work in a way that is friendly to the world around us.

It is a big task.

13

Day and night

Day and Night Facts

◆ The Sun rises and sets 12 minutes later in Bristol than in London, for example.
◆ Over large distances time differences become greater and so we have time zones.
◆ When it is 6pm in London it is 4am the next day in Sydney and 10am the same day in Los Angeles.

The Earth spins through one complete turn in a day. This produces sunrise, daylight, sunset and night.

Spinning Earth

The spinning of the Earth is what gives us our day. It takes 24 hours for the Earth to make one complete spin.

From the ground, it is not easy to see that the Earth is spinning at all. Instead, we get the impression that the Earth remains still, while the Sun appears to rise in the east and fall towards the west each day (pictures ① and ②).

Sunrise

Because the Earth is spinning, different parts of the Earth receive sunlight at different times of the day.

When you wake up and see the sunrise, the part of the Earth where you are standing turns out of the shadow (it was in shadow because it was facing away from the Sun) and begins to turn towards the Sun (picture ②A).

You see this as the Sun rising above the horizon in the eastern part of the sky.

Daylight

Daylight lasts for as long as our part of the Earth is turned towards the Sun. As the morning passes, the Earth turns to face the Sun more directly (picture ②B). We see this as the Sun rising in the sky.

The Sun is highest in the sky at midday, or noon (picture ②C).

Sunset

After midday, the part of the Earth where we are begins to turn away from the Sun. We see this as the Sun sinking in the sky towards the west (picture ②D). As the Earth finally turns away from the Sun, the Sun appears to set.

Night

While the part of the Earth where we are is turned away from the Sun we are in shadow, so darkness, or night, occurs.

▼ ① **The spinning of the Earth causes different parts of the Earth to receive sunlight at different times of the day.**

▼ ② **The Sun appears to move in a curve across the sky, rising at dawn, then reaching its highest at midday, before sinking at sunset.**

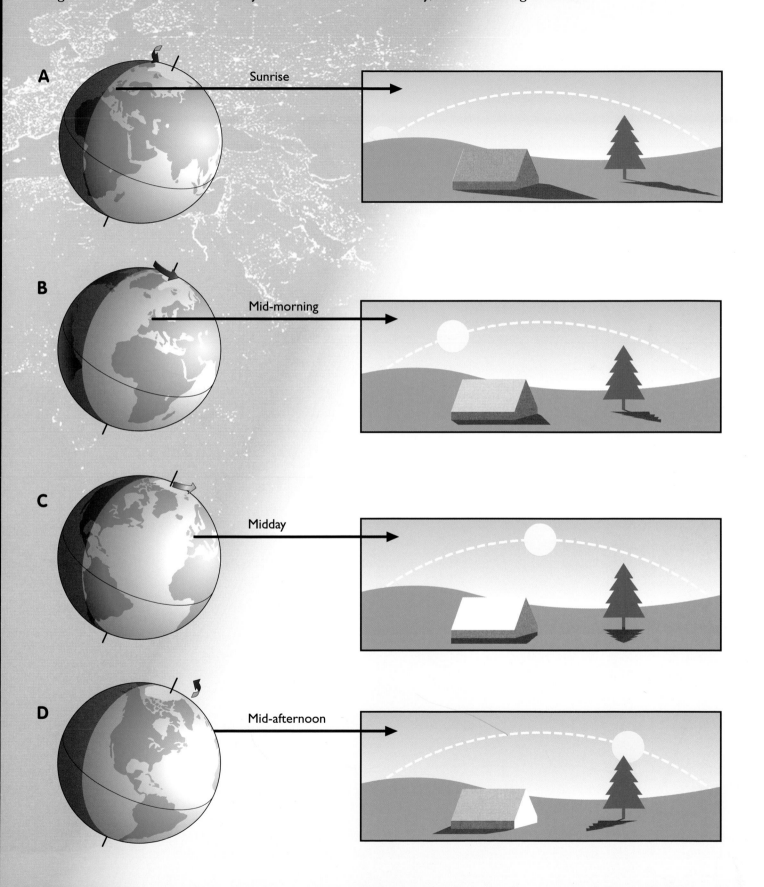

A — Sunrise

B — Mid-morning

C — Midday

D — Mid-afternoon

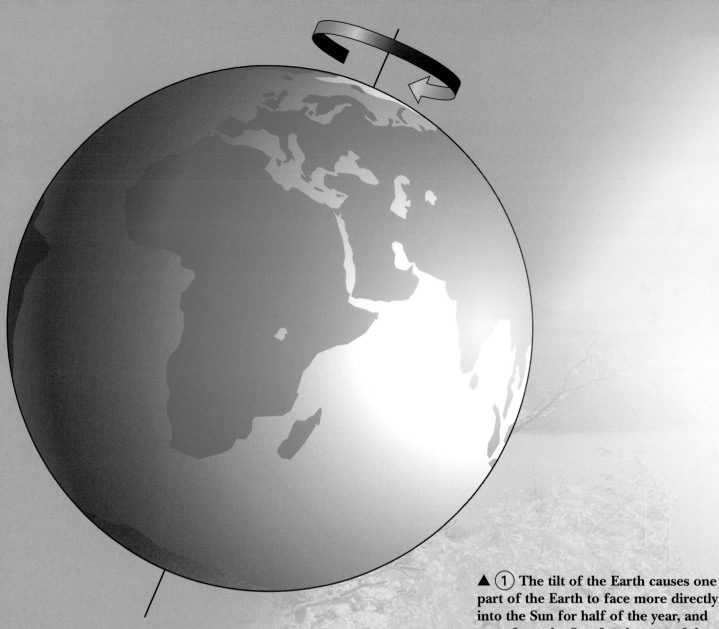

▲ ① The tilt of the Earth causes one part of the Earth to face more directly into the Sun for half of the year, and away from the Sun for the rest of the year. This tilt causes the seasons.

Seasons

The Earth goes around the Sun once a year. This produces the seasons – spring, summer, autumn and winter.

The Earth moves in two ways – it tilts as it spins, and it travels around the Sun. These two movements give us our seasons – spring, summer, autumn and winter.

Tilted Earth

The key to the seasons is the way the Earth is slightly tilted onto its side as it spins (picture ①).

This tilt causes one part of the Earth to face more directly into the sunlight. This is summer. Meanwhile, the other part of the Earth is less directly in the sunlight. This is winter (picture ②).

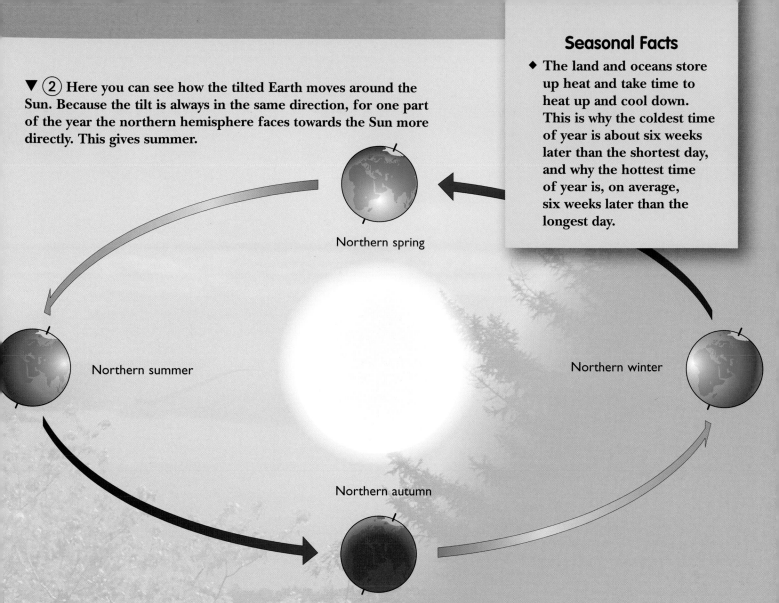

▼ ② Here you can see how the tilted Earth moves around the Sun. Because the tilt is always in the same direction, for one part of the year the northern hemisphere faces towards the Sun more directly. This gives summer.

Northern spring

Northern summer

Northern winter

Northern autumn

Summer

When the northern part of the Earth is tilted more directly towards the Sun it gets more sunlight each day. The Sun shines for a longer time each day and rises higher in the sky. This means that more sunshine reaches that part of the Earth and it gets hotter. This is summer in the northern half of the Earth.

Winter

When the northern part of the Earth is tilted away from the Sun it gets less sunlight each day. The Sun shines for a shorter time each day and rises less high in the sky. This means that the northern part of the Earth does not get much warmth. This is winter.

Spring and autumn

Spring and autumn are half way stages in the orbit of the Earth. They are the times when all parts of the Earth have equal day and night. This happens because the Earth is facing sideways to the Sun, with neither northern nor southern hemispheres having more sunshine.

Weblink: www.CurriculumVisions.com

▲ ① How the Moon looks from the Earth. Notice that we see the Moon through our atmosphere. The picture gives a Space Shuttle view, showing the atmosphere very clearly.

▲▶ ② Notice the craters that have been formed by collisions with asteroids. There are also very large dark areas. These are called seas, although they have no water. The large one in the centre is called the Sea of Tranquillity. It seems to be filled with lava rock. (Right) A close-up of the Moon's cratered surface.

Moon

Our Moon is the largest in the Solar System compared to the size of its planet.

You could hardly think of two more different places than the Earth and the Moon (picture ①).

But the Moon and the Earth have something in common: they were probably once part of the same planet.

Soon after the Earth had formed, another small planet probably crashed into the Earth, shattering itself and knocking off part of the Earth. The dust and chunks of rock then started to circle the Earth, gradually coming together to form the Moon.

At this time the centre of the Moon may have been **MOLTEN** and **VOLCANOES** may have sent **LAVA** over parts of the surface. However, any volcanoes are now extinct and the Moon shows no active surface at all.

The Moon has no **ATMOSPHERE** and so all **ASTEROIDS** hit the surface, covering it with deep **CRATERS** (picture ②). This is how we see the surface today (pictures ③ and ④).

Half Moon

Waxing gibbous Moon

Waxing: to get bigger
Waning: to get smaller

Waxing crescent Moon

Full Moon

Earth

New Moon

Waning gibbous Moon

Half Moon

Waning crescent Moon

Moon Facts

◆ The Moon is 384,400 km from the Earth.
◆ The Moon is 3,476 km across.
◆ The Moon always shows the same side to the Earth because it spins around in 29.5 days, the same time as it takes to go around the Earth.
◆ Some craters are more than 300 km across.

◀ ③ The amount of the Moon we see depends on how much sunlight bounces from its surface.

It varies from a whole disc (a full Moon) to no Moon at all. The changing patterns are called the phases of the Moon.

▼ ④ This dramatic picture shows a Moon Rover vehicle on the Moon's surface.

The soil is also dry as dust, lifeless and thin. Look at the bootprints. You can see the sides of a crater in the background. Notice the sky is black because there is no atmosphere. (For more information on the Moon, see the companion book *Journey into space*.

Weblink: www.CurriculumVisions.com

Size of the Moon and Sun

The Earth is about four times as wide as the Moon. The Sun is about 100 times as wide as the Earth. But from Earth the Moon appears to be about the same size as the Sun.

When looking into the sky, things may not appear the size they really are. Vast objects, like the Sun, seem the same size as much smaller objects, like the Moon, (picture ①).

Optical illusion

When something appears to be different from what it really is, it is called an optical illusion.

The size an object appears to be depends on how much of our view it takes up.

To understand this, hold a pencil close to your face and then at arm's length (picture ②). The further away

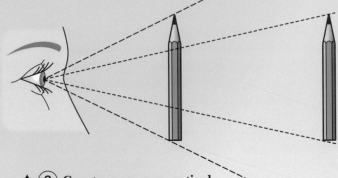

▲ ② **Create your own optical illusion.** Try holding two pencils, which are the same height, at different distances apart. Do they still look the same size?

the pencil is, the smaller it appears to be. Of course, we know the pencil is the same size far away as it was when it was close. The difference in size is an optical illusion.

Moon

Sun

◀▼ ① The way we see things can create an optical illusion. When we see both the Moon and the Sun together in the sky, they appear to be about the same size. You can see this in the partial eclipse picture below.

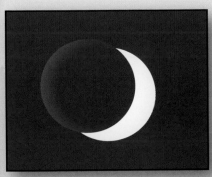

Size Facts

- The Sun is almost 1,400,000 kilometres across.
- The Earth is nearly 13,000 kilometres across, just a hundredth of the diameter of the Sun.
- The Moon is 3,500 kilometres across, only a quarter of the diameter of the Earth (pictures ⑤ and ⑥).

When we look at the Moon and the Sun we cannot easily see that one is closer than the other, so even though the Moon is much smaller than the Sun, it appears to be about the same size (pictures ③ and ④).

▼ ③ The Moon is closer to the Earth than the Sun. This is why it looks about the same size as the Sun.

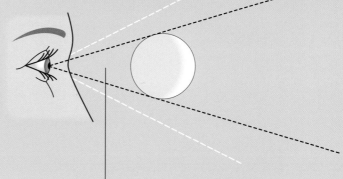

These angles are the same.

▼ ④ The Sun is much bigger than the Moon, but because it is so much farther away, it appears to be a similar size to the Moon.

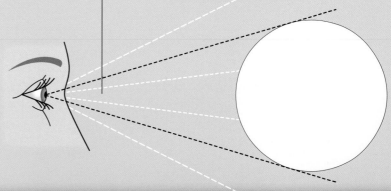

▲ ⑤ Here is the Earth seen with the Moon in about their correct proportions, the Earth being four times the diameter of the Moon.

▼ ⑥ Another illusion. The Moon is much smaller than the Earth, but when you see the Earth from the Moon, it is the Earth that appears small!

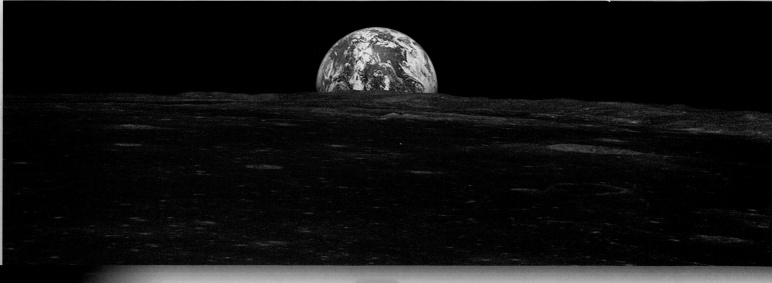

21

Shadows and eclipses

When sunlight is blocked, it casts a shadow. This is true both for small objects, like a tree, and for large ones, like the Moon.

Sunlight travels in straight lines and cannot bend around objects. This is why, when sunlight is blocked by an object like a tree or a stick, it casts a **SHADOW** away from the Sun (picture ①).

Shadow direction

The direction of the shadow depends on where the Sun is in the sky. In the morning, the Sun is in the east and so the shadow lies to the west; in the evening the Sun is in the west and so the shadow lies to the east (picture ②). In the northern hemisphere, the Sun shines out from the southern half of the sky so the shadow also lies slightly to the north.

▶ ① Long shadows cast by the early morning Sun as it is blocked by some trees.

▼ ② How the length and direction of the Sun's shadow change through the day. (Here we have our back to the Sun. Compare this to picture ②, page 15, where we are facing the Sun.)

Shadow length

Shadows change length depending on the height of the Sun in the sky. In the morning and evening the Sun is low and the shadows are long. Near to midday the shadows are much shorter.

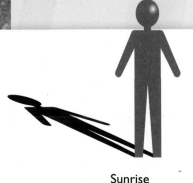  

Sunrise   Mid-morning   Midday   Mid-afternoon

Eclipse

An **ECLIPSE** occurs when a body in space, like the Moon, goes in between the Earth and another body, like the Sun (pictures ③ and ④). When the Moon gets between the Earth and the Sun it gives a solar eclipse. When the Earth gets between the Moon and the Sun it gives a lunar eclipse.

In a solar eclipse, the Moon is just big enough to block out sunlight over a small part of the Earth. Outside this small part, some or all of the sunlight can still be seen.

Eclipse Facts

- Eclipses of the Sun occur at times of the New Moon.
- Eclipses of the Moon occur at times of the Full Moon.
- Eclipses are rare because the Moon orbits the Earth in a different direction from the way the Earth orbits the Sun.
- Solar eclipses occur in the day.
- Lunar eclipses occur at night.

Sun

Moon

Earth

Umbra

Penumbra

◀ ③ When an eclipse occurs, the Moon appears to completely cover the Sun over a small part of the Earth. This is a total eclipse, and that part of the Earth in line with the Moon is in deep shadow. In places close by, the Moon appears to cover only part of the Sun so only some shade occurs. In these places people see a partial eclipse.

▼ ④ As the Moon passed between the Sun and the Earth in August 1999, a satellite took this picture of the eclipse over the Mediterranean Sea and Africa.

Sunset

Weblink: www.CurriculumVisions.com

Index

Curriculum Visions

*Curriculum Visions is a registered trademark of
Atlantic Europe Publishing Company Ltd.*

Atlantic Europe Publishing

First published in 2004 by
Atlantic Europe Publishing Company Ltd

Copyright © 2004
Atlantic Europe Publishing Company Ltd

Author
Brian Knapp, BSc, PhD

Art Director
Duncan McCrae, BSc

Senior Designer
Adele Humphries, BA, PGCE

Editors
Lisa Magloff, MA, and Gillian Gatehouse

Illustrations on behalf of Earthscape Editions
David Woodroffe and David Hardy

Designed and produced by
EARTHSCAPE EDITIONS

Printed in China by
WKT Company Ltd.

Spaceship Earth – *Curriculum Visions*
A CIP record for this book is available
from the British Library.

Paperback ISBN 1 86214 388 9
Hardback ISBN 1 86214 389 7

Acknowledgements
Dodo sculpture picture on page 12 courtesy
of Gallery Pangolin and sculptor Nick Bibby.

Picture credits
All photographs courtesy of NASA, except
the following: (c=centre t=top b=bottom l=left
r=right) *Earthscape Editions* 6, 7t, 8, 9, 10t, 12t,
12cr, 12br, 13, 15, 16, 17, 20t, 20b, 21cr, 22cr,
22–23b; *Space Imaging* 11tr; *Syndics of Cambridge
University Library* 12bl; *USGS (Austin Post)* 7b.

*This product is manufactured from sustainable
managed forests. For every tree cut down at least
one more is planted.*

The Curriculum Visions web site
Details of our other products can be found at:

www.CurriculumVisions.com